Cultivating a Sustainable Future: Principles and Practices of Regenerative Agriculture

As our world continues to grapple with pressing issues like climate change, soil degradation, and food insecurity, it's become increasingly clear that our agricultural systems must change. We need a new approach that prioritizes the health of the land, the resilience of local communities, and the sustainability of our food systems. This is where regenerative agriculture comes in.

Regenerative agriculture seeks to restore, rather than deplete, the natural resources that are critical to agricultural productivity. It emphasizes the importance of biodiversity, soil health, and ecological balance, while also promoting economic viability for farmers and their communities. Through a combination of traditional and innovative practices, regenerative agriculture has the potential to revolutionize the way we farm and feed the world.

In this book, we'll explore the principles and practices of regenerative agriculture in depth, from cover cropping and crop rotation to agroforestry and no-till farming. We'll examine the environmental, economic, and social benefits of regenerative agriculture, as well as the challenges and opportunities facing farmers, policymakers, and communities as they work to implement sustainable farming practices. Through case studies, interviews, and expert analysis, we'll show how regenerative agriculture can transform our food systems, create more resilient communities, and nurture a sustainable future for generations to come.

I. Introduction

Definition Of Sustainable Farming

Sustainable farming is an agricultural method that emphasizes the use of natural resources in a way that conserves and protects them for future generations while also ensuring the long-term viability of the farm operation. This involves using techniques that minimize harm to the environment, promoting biodiversity, reducing the use of non-renewable resources, and maximizing the productivity and profitability of the farm. Sustainable farming practices aim to balance environmental, economic, and social considerations to create a system that is sustainable over the long term.

The Importance Of Sustainable Farming In Today's World

Sustainable farming is increasingly important in today's world as the global population continues to grow, and there is greater demand for food production. With traditional farming practices, the environment, and natural resources are often exploited, leading to soil degradation, loss of biodiversity, and pollution of waterways. Sustainable farming practices seek to address these issues by promoting techniques that are environmentally friendly, socially responsible, and economically viable.

Sustainable farming is crucial for ensuring food security, protecting natural resources, and reducing greenhouse gas emissions. As we face climate change, soil erosion, and water scarcity, sustainable farming practices offer an alternative that can help to mitigate these challenges. Additionally, sustainable farming practices help to create healthier ecosystems, which can support not only crops and livestock but also other wildlife.

Sustainable farming practices also offer economic benefits for farmers and their communities. These practices can reduce input costs, increase yields, and improve the quality of crops and livestock, leading to higher profits. By investing in sustainable farming, farmers can also create more stable livelihoods, which can help to strengthen local economies.

In summary, sustainable farming practices are essential for ensuring long-term food security, protecting the environment, and supporting the economic and social well-being of farmers and their communities.

II. Principles of Sustainable Farming

Regenerative Farming Practices

Regenerative farming practices are a set of principles and practices that seek to revitalize and regenerate the natural resources and ecosystems that support agricultural production. These practices aim to create healthy, resilient, and productive agricultural systems that benefit both farmers and the environment. Some common regenerative farming practices include:

Conservation Tillage: This practice involves leaving crop residues on the soil surface and reducing or eliminating tillage to improve soil health and reduce erosion.

Cover Cropping: Cover crops are grown between cash crops to improve soil health, reduce erosion, and increase nutrient retention.

Crop Rotation: Rotating crops on a regular basis helps to break pest cycles, reduce soil-borne diseases, and improve soil health.

Regenerative Grazing: This practice involves managing livestock in a way that mimics the natural movement and grazing patterns of wild herbivores.

Agroforestry: Agroforestry involves integrating trees and shrubs into agricultural landscapes to improve soil health, increase biodiversity, and provide additional sources of income.

Intercropping: Intercropping involves growing two or more crops in the same field to improve soil health, reduce pest pressure, and increase yields.

No-till Farming: No-till farming involves planting crops directly into undisturbed soil, which helps to reduce soil erosion and improve soil health.

These practices are based on the principles of ecological stewardship, which emphasize the importance of working with natural systems rather than against them. By using regenerative farming practices, farmers can improve soil health, reduce the use of synthetic inputs, increase biodiversity, and improve their bottom line. Additionally, these practices can help to address some of the environmental and social challenges facing our planet, such as climate change, soil erosion, and food insecurity.

Minimizing Negative Impacts On Ecosystems

Sustainable farming practices aim to minimize the negative impacts of agriculture on the surrounding ecosystems. This can be achieved by using less harmful pesticides and fertilizers, reducing tillage practices, and managing soil erosion. Another way to minimize negative impacts is to conserve natural habitats, such as wetlands, forests, and grasslands, that are vital for biodiversity and provide ecological services such as water purification, soil formation, and carbon sequestration. Additionally, sustainable farming practices can incorporate techniques such as agroforestry, cover cropping, crop rotation, no-till farming, and intercropping, which promote soil health and fertility, increase biodiversity, and reduce greenhouse gas emissions.

Biodiversity And Crop Rotation

Biodiversity and crop rotation are two important practices in sustainable farming that can improve soil health, prevent soil erosion, and reduce the need for synthetic fertilizers and pesticides.

Biodiversity refers to the variety of plant and animal species in an ecosystem. In agriculture, increasing biodiversity can involve growing a greater diversity of crops and incorporating natural areas such as hedgerows, buffer strips, and wetlands into the farm landscape. This can provide habitat for beneficial insects and other wildlife, and help to control pests and diseases naturally. Additionally, diverse crop rotations can help to break pest and disease cycles, increase soil organic matter, and improve soil structure and fertility.

Crop rotation involves growing different crops in a specific sequence on a piece of land over time. This can help to prevent soil depletion, control pests and diseases, and improve soil fertility. For example, legume crops such as peas and beans can fix nitrogen from the air and improve soil nitrogen levels for subsequent crops. Crop rotations can also help to reduce erosion and nutrient runoff by providing year-round ground cover.

Both biodiversity and crop rotation can be enhanced through the use of cover crops, which are grown specifically to benefit the soil rather than for harvest. Cover crops can help to prevent soil erosion, increase soil organic matter, and improve soil fertility by fixing nitrogen, scavenging nutrients, and breaking up compacted soil. They can also provide habitat for beneficial insects and wildlife.

Overall, promoting biodiversity and crop rotation can help to improve the sustainability and resilience of farming systems, while reducing their negative impacts on the environment.

Local Adaptation

Local adaptation in sustainable farming refers to the practice of developing farming systems that are specifically designed to work in the local context. This involves considering factors such as the climate, soil type, and available resources when choosing crops, livestock, and farming methods. By adapting to local conditions, farmers can create more resilient and sustainable systems that are better equipped to deal with challenges such as drought, flooding, and pest outbreaks. Local adaptation also takes into account the social and cultural context of the farming community, including traditional knowledge and practices. This helps to ensure that sustainable farming practices are not only effective but also acceptable and accessible to local farmers.

III. Sustainable Farming Techniques

Integrated Pest Management

Integrated pest management (IPM) is a sustainable approach to managing pests and diseases that can damage crops. It combines different methods and strategies to control pests in a way that is both effective and environmentally friendly. IPM methods include biological control (using natural predators and parasites to control pests), cultural practices (such as crop rotation and intercropping to reduce pest pressure), physical control (such as trapping and barrier methods), and chemical control (using pesticides only when necessary and in a targeted manner). IPM aims to minimize the use of harmful pesticides and promote the use of non-toxic and non-polluting alternatives, while also protecting natural enemies of pests and reducing the risk of developing resistance to pesticides.

Organic Farming Methods

Organic farming is a method of sustainable agriculture that avoids the use of synthetic pesticides and fertilizers and relies on natural methods of pest and weed control. It also emphasizes the use of organic matter and soil conservation to maintain soil fertility and reduce erosion. Organic farming practices include crop rotation, intercropping, composting, and cover cropping. Organic farmers also prioritize the health and welfare of their animals and do not use antibiotics or growth hormones. Organic farming has been shown to produce yields comparable to conventional farming methods while also improving soil health and reducing environmental pollution.

Agroforestry

Agroforestry is a sustainable land management system that involves the integration of trees and shrubs with crops and/or livestock on the same piece of land. This approach enhances the ecological, economic, and social functions of the farming system by promoting biodiversity, soil health, nutrient cycling, and climate resilience.

In agroforestry, the trees and shrubs can be used to provide various benefits such as windbreaks, shade, and shelter for livestock, as well as food, fodder, fuel, and timber for human use. Agroforestry systems can be designed to suit the specific needs and conditions of a particular region or community, and can range from simple intercropping of trees and crops to complex multilayered systems with diverse plant and animal species.

The use of agroforestry practices can lead to multiple benefits, such as reduced soil erosion, improved water quality, increased carbon sequestration, enhanced biodiversity, and increased income for farmers. By integrating trees and shrubs into their farming systems, farmers can also diversify their income streams and reduce their dependence on single crops, thus improving their economic resilience.

Conservation Tillage

Conservation tillage is a sustainable farming technique that involves reducing or eliminating tillage operations, which are the mechanical manipulation of soil used to prepare it for planting or weed control. Conservation tillage techniques include no-till farming, reduced tillage, and strip tillage, which can help to improve soil health, reduce soil erosion and water loss, and increase the efficiency of fertilizer and pesticide use. By reducing tillage, conservation tillage practices can also help to preserve soil structure and increase soil organic matter, which can enhance soil fertility and support healthier plant growth. Conservation tillage is becoming increasingly popular among farmers around the world as a way to reduce their environmental impact and improve the sustainability of their farming practices.

Drip Irrigation

Drip irrigation is a type of micro-irrigation system that delivers water directly to the root zone of plants, drop by drop, through a network of pipes and emitters. This method of irrigation is highly efficient and can save significant amounts of water compared to traditional flood irrigation methods, which can result in high rates of water evaporation and runoff. Drip irrigation also allows for precise control of water delivery, which can improve crop yields and reduce the risk of plant diseases associated with overwatering. Additionally, drip irrigation systems can be used in a variety of farming systems, including row crops, orchards, and vineyards. Overall, drip irrigation is a sustainable and effective method of providing plants with the water they need to grow and thrive, while conserving water resources and reducing the negative impacts of irrigation on the environment.

IV. Sustainable Livestock Farming

Grazing Techniques That Promote Biodiversity

Grazing techniques that promote biodiversity are essential for sustainable farming. The following are some examples:

Rotational grazing: Rotational grazing involves moving livestock from one pasture to another, giving each pasture a rest period to recover before it is grazed again. This method helps to promote biodiversity by allowing plant species to recover and flourish.

Silvopasture: Silvopasture is a method of combining livestock grazing with tree cultivation. This method provides shade and shelter for livestock, while also promoting the growth of trees and other plants. It can help to improve soil health, prevent erosion, and increase biodiversity.

High-density grazing: High-density grazing involves grazing livestock on a small area of land for a short period of time. This method helps to promote biodiversity by encouraging plant growth and increasing soil fertility.

Managed intensive grazing: Managed intensive grazing involves grazing livestock on a small area of land for a short period of time, then moving them to a new area. This method helps to promote biodiversity by allowing the land to rest and recover between grazing periods.

Conservation grazing: Conservation grazing involves using livestock to manage and restore habitats such as grasslands, wetlands, and heathlands. This method can help to increase biodiversity by promoting the growth of native plant species and creating habitats for wildlife.

By incorporating these grazing techniques into their farming practices, farmers can help to promote biodiversity, improve soil health, and increase the sustainability of their operations.

Animal Welfare Considerations

Animal welfare considerations in sustainable farming focus on ensuring that animals are treated ethically and humanely. This includes providing them with adequate food, water, and shelter, as well as proper healthcare and protection from predators or extreme weather conditions. Farmers who practice sustainable farming also ensure that animals have access to space to move and exercise, as well as a natural environment where they can exhibit their natural behaviors. The goal is to raise animals in a manner that meets their biological needs while minimizing their stress and discomfort. In addition to animal welfare, sustainable farming practices also aim to reduce the environmental impact of livestock farming, such as minimizing waste, reducing greenhouse gas emissions, and preserving soil health.

Alternative Protein Sources

Alternative protein sources are non-traditional sources of protein that can supplement or replace traditional animal-based protein sources like beef, pork, and chicken. These alternative sources can include plant-based protein sources such as soy, beans, and lentils, as well as other sources like algae, insects, and lab-grown meat.

The production of animal-based protein sources can have significant environmental impacts, such as deforestation, greenhouse gas emissions, and water pollution. The use of alternative protein sources can help to reduce these impacts and make food systems more sustainable.

Plant-based protein sources are often more resource-efficient than animal-based sources, requiring less land, water, and energy to produce. Insects, which are a common protein source in many parts of the world, can also be a more sustainable option than traditional livestock, as they require fewer resources and produce fewer greenhouse gas emissions.

Lab-grown meat, also known as cultured meat, is an emerging technology that involves growing meat in a laboratory from animal cells. This technology has the potential to provide a sustainable alternative to traditional meat production, as it requires fewer resources and produces fewer greenhouse gas emissions.

Overall, the use of alternative protein sources has the potential to help create a more sustainable and resilient food system that is better equipped to meet the challenges of the future.

V. Sustainable Farming in Different Regions

Sustainable Farming Practices In North America

Sustainable farming practices have been gaining traction in North America in recent years, as farmers and consumers alike recognize the importance of sustainable agriculture in promoting both environmental and human health.

One such practice is crop rotation, which involves growing different crops in a particular field in a planned sequence over several seasons. This helps to minimize soil erosion and nutrient depletion, and can also reduce the incidence of pests and diseases.

Another sustainable farming practice is no-till farming, which avoids disturbing the soil by plowing or tilling. This helps to preserve soil structure and moisture content, reduce erosion, and decrease the carbon footprint of farming operations.

Conservation tillage, which involves minimal disturbance of the soil, is also becoming more popular among sustainable farmers. This method can reduce soil erosion and nutrient depletion, while still allowing for the planting of crops.

Grazing management is another important aspect of sustainable farming, and can involve rotational grazing, multi-species grazing, and other practices that help to promote biodiversity and improve soil health.

Finally, many sustainable farmers in North America are turning to agroforestry, which involves integrating trees and shrubs into agricultural landscapes. This can help to reduce soil erosion, increase biodiversity, and provide other environmental and economic benefits.

Overall, sustainable farming practices are becoming increasingly important in North America, as farmers and consumers recognize the need to promote environmental health and sustainability while still producing high-quality food for local communities.

Sustainable Farming Practices In Europe

In Europe, sustainable farming practices have gained prominence in recent years, partly due to the implementation of policies aimed at promoting sustainable agriculture. The Common Agricultural Policy (CAP) of the European Union, for instance, incentivizes farmers to adopt sustainable practices through various measures, such as direct payments for environmental and climate-related actions, and support for organic farming.

One example of sustainable farming practices in Europe is agroecology, which involves the application of ecological principles to farming systems. Agroecological practices such as crop diversification, intercropping, and the use of natural pest control methods help to promote biodiversity and reduce the reliance on synthetic inputs.

Another example is precision farming, which involves the use of technology to optimize crop yields while reducing environmental impacts. Precision farming techniques include the use of GPS mapping to identify variations in soil fertility and moisture levels, and the use of sensors to monitor crop growth and health.

Organic farming is also increasingly popular in Europe, with countries such as Austria, Sweden, and Italy having the highest proportion of organic farmland. Organic farming practices involve the use of natural inputs and the avoidance of synthetic pesticides and fertilizers, resulting in reduced environmental impacts and improved soil health.

In addition, there are various initiatives in Europe aimed at promoting sustainable food systems, such as local food networks and community-supported agriculture (CSA) schemes. These initiatives help to reduce food miles and support local farmers, while also promoting more sustainable consumption patterns.

Sustainable Farming Practices In Asia

Sustainable farming practices in Asia vary greatly due to the continent's vast size and diverse climates, cultures, and agricultural traditions. However, there are several notable examples of sustainable farming practices in Asia:

Rice-fish farming: In China, Vietnam, and other Asian countries, farmers practice rice-fish farming, where fish are raised in the flooded rice paddies. This practice not only provides an additional source of protein for the farmers but also helps control pests and weeds in the rice fields.

Agroforestry: Agroforestry practices, such as planting fruit and nut trees alongside crops, are common in Southeast Asia. In Indonesia, for example, farmers practice the "tumpangsari" system, where fruit and nut trees are grown alongside cash crops like coffee and cocoa.

Terrace farming: Terrace farming, which involves creating flat fields on steep hillsides, is a common practice in many parts of Asia. This technique helps prevent soil erosion and allows farmers to cultivate crops on land that might otherwise be unusable.

Organic farming: Organic farming is gaining popularity in Asia, particularly in countries like India, where farmers are increasingly turning to organic methods to combat soil degradation and declining yields.

Small-scale farming: Small-scale farming is prevalent in many parts of Asia, particularly in rural areas. This type of farming often relies on traditional techniques and local knowledge, and can be highly sustainable if managed properly.

Sustainable Farming Practices In Africa

Africa is a vast continent with diverse climatic zones and agricultural practices. There are many sustainable farming practices that are being implemented across the continent. Some examples include:

Agroforestry: Agroforestry is a sustainable farming technique that integrates trees with crops and/or livestock to create a more diverse and productive agricultural system. In Africa, agroforestry is being used to restore degraded lands, increase soil fertility, and provide food and income for rural communities.

Conservation agriculture: Conservation agriculture is a farming system that aims to conserve soil, water, and biodiversity while increasing yields and improving livelihoods. In Africa, conservation agriculture is being used to reduce soil erosion, improve water retention, and enhance soil fertility.

Organic farming: Organic farming is a farming system that relies on natural processes and inputs to produce crops and livestock. In Africa, organic farming is being used to improve soil fertility, reduce reliance on external inputs, and produce healthier and more nutritious food.

Permaculture: Permaculture is a holistic approach to farming that seeks to create sustainable and self-sufficient ecosystems. In Africa, permaculture is being used to restore degraded lands, increase biodiversity, and provide food and income for local communities.

Water harvesting: Water harvesting is a technique that involves collecting and storing rainwater for use in agriculture. In Africa, water harvesting is being used to increase crop yields, reduce dependence on erratic rainfall, and improve livelihoods in arid and semi-arid areas.

These are just a few examples of sustainable farming practices being implemented in Africa. Despite the challenges faced by many farmers on the continent, there is a growing movement towards more sustainable and regenerative agricultural practices that can help build resilient and prosperous communities.

Sustainable Farming Practices In South America

South America has a diverse range of ecosystems, from the Amazon rainforest to the Andes mountains to the grasslands of the Pampas. As such, sustainable farming practices vary depending on the region and climate. However, some general sustainable farming practices in South America include:

Agroforestry: Integrating trees into farming systems, which can provide shade, windbreaks, and erosion control, while also providing food and timber.

Crop rotation and cover cropping: Alternating different crops and using cover crops can help maintain soil fertility and prevent erosion.

Conservation tillage: Reducing soil disturbance during planting and cultivation can help retain moisture and reduce erosion.

Integrated pest management: Using a variety of methods, such as crop rotation, intercropping, and biological control, to manage pests and reduce the need for pesticides.

Organic farming: Avoiding synthetic pesticides and fertilizers, and instead relying on natural inputs and soil-building practices.

Sustainable grazing: Using managed grazing techniques that promote biodiversity, such as rotational grazing and the restoration of grasslands.

Water conservation: Implementing irrigation systems that reduce water waste and using drought-resistant crops.

Many small-scale farmers in South America also practice agroecology, which involves integrating ecological principles into farming practices to promote biodiversity and ecosystem health.

VI. Challenges and Opportunities in Sustainable Farming

Economic Challenges And Opportunities

Sustainable farming practices can offer a range of economic benefits, such as reducing input costs, increasing yields, and improving the quality of produce. However, there can also be economic challenges associated with transitioning to sustainable farming, such as the cost of implementing new practices, the need for specialized knowledge and training, and potentially lower yields during the transition period.

One opportunity for sustainable farming is the growing demand for sustainably-produced food among consumers. This can lead to higher prices for sustainably-produced products, as well as increased demand for local and regional food systems that support small-scale and diversified farming operations.

In addition, sustainable farming practices can also create opportunities for new and innovative business models, such as community-supported agriculture (CSA) and direct-to-consumer marketing channels, which can provide farmers with more control over the pricing and distribution of their products.

However, sustainable farming still faces challenges in terms of access to capital and resources, as well as competition from industrial-scale farming operations that can produce food at a lower cost. Policymakers and stakeholders need to work together to create supportive policies and incentives that can help farmers transition to sustainable farming practices while maintaining their livelihoods.

Policy Challenges And Opportunities

There are several policy challenges and opportunities that impact the adoption and success of sustainable farming practices.

One of the main challenges is the lack of government support for sustainable farming. Many agricultural policies and subsidies are geared towards conventional farming practices that prioritize high yields and production over sustainability. This creates an uneven playing field for sustainable farmers who may not have access to the same financial resources and support.

Another challenge is the lack of regulation and enforcement around environmental standards in agriculture. Sustainable farming practices often prioritize environmental conservation and protection, but without proper regulation and enforcement, there is little incentive for farmers to adopt these practices.

However, there are also opportunities for policy change and support for sustainable farming practices. Some governments and organizations are starting to recognize the importance of sustainable agriculture and are investing in research, education, and financial support for farmers. There are also efforts to reform agricultural policies and subsidies to better support sustainable farming practices.

In addition, consumer demand for sustainably produced food is growing, which creates a market opportunity for farmers who adopt sustainable practices. This can be encouraged and supported by policies that promote labeling and certification for sustainably produced foods.

Overall, there is a need for policy makers to recognize the importance of sustainable farming practices and to create policies and regulations that support their adoption and success.

Social Challenges And Opportunities

Social challenges and opportunities are also important aspects of sustainable farming. Some of the social challenges in sustainable farming include the high costs of adopting sustainable practices, lack of access to resources and information, and resistance to change from traditional farming practices. Additionally, there can be challenges in creating equitable and fair labor practices, especially in large-scale agricultural operations.

However, sustainable farming also provides social opportunities, such as creating stronger connections between farmers and their local communities. Sustainable farming can also create more job opportunities in local communities, and it can help to preserve and promote traditional knowledge and cultures related to agriculture. Sustainable farming can also contribute to better health outcomes, as sustainably grown produce is often fresher and more nutritious than conventionally grown produce.

Technological Challenges And Opportunities

Advancements in technology have a significant impact on sustainable farming practices. Emerging technologies can help farmers increase yields, reduce costs, and minimize negative environmental impacts. For example, precision agriculture tools like sensors, drones, and GPS mapping can help farmers make more informed decisions about planting and harvesting, reducing waste and improving efficiency. Additionally, biotechnology and genetic engineering can help farmers develop crops that are more resistant to pests, diseases, and drought.

However, there are also challenges associated with the adoption of new technologies. Some farmers may not have access to the necessary resources or training to effectively utilize these tools, and there may be concerns about the safety and long-term effects of genetically modified crops.

Overall, technology presents both challenges and opportunities for sustainable farming practices. As new technologies emerge, it is important to consider their potential impacts on the environment, farmers, and society as a whole.

VII. *The Future of Sustainable Farming*

The Potential For Sustainable Farming To Address Global Challenges

Sustainable farming has the potential to address a range of global challenges, including:

Climate change: Sustainable farming practices can reduce greenhouse gas emissions, increase carbon sequestration, and improve soil health, which can help mitigate the impacts of climate change.

Food security: Sustainable farming practices can increase the productivity and resilience of agricultural systems, which can help ensure that enough food is produced to feed the world's growing population.

Biodiversity conservation: Sustainable farming practices can help protect and enhance biodiversity by promoting the use of diverse crop and livestock species, maintaining natural habitats, and reducing the use of harmful chemicals.

Water conservation and quality: Sustainable farming practices can help conserve water resources by promoting more efficient use of water and reducing pollution of waterways.

Economic development: Sustainable farming practices can provide economic benefits for farmers and rural communities by increasing productivity, reducing costs, and enhancing the quality and value of agricultural products.

Overall, sustainable farming offers a holistic approach to agricultural production that takes into account the interconnectedness of social, economic, and environmental factors. By adopting sustainable farming practices, we can create a more resilient, equitable, and sustainable food system that benefits people and the planet.

Advances In Sustainable Farming Technology

There are several advances in sustainable farming technology that are currently being developed and implemented. Here are some examples:

Precision agriculture: This involves using data and technology to make more informed decisions about crop management. Farmers can use sensors, drones, and other tools to monitor soil moisture, crop growth, and nutrient levels. This allows them to make more targeted use of resources such as water and fertilizer, reducing waste and increasing efficiency.

Vertical farming: This involves growing crops in stacked layers using artificial light, often in urban environments. This approach can increase crop yields while using less land and water than traditional farming methods.

Biotechnology: This involves using genetic engineering and other techniques to develop crops that are more resistant to pests and diseases, or that require less water or fertilizer. While controversial, biotechnology has the potential to increase crop yields and reduce the use of harmful chemicals.

Robotics and automation: This involves using machines and robots to perform tasks such as planting, harvesting, and weeding. This can increase efficiency and reduce the need for manual labor, which can be a challenge for many farmers.

Renewable energy: This involves using solar, wind, or other renewable energy sources to power farming operations. This can reduce greenhouse gas emissions and make farms more self-sufficient.

Overall, these and other advances in sustainable farming technology have the potential to make farming more efficient, environmentally friendly, and economically viable.

The Role Of Farmers, Policymakers, And Consumers In Promoting Sustainable Farming

The role of farmers, policymakers, and consumers is critical in promoting sustainable farming. Farmers can adopt sustainable farming practices and methods on their farms, which can have positive impacts on the environment and their communities. Policymakers can support sustainable farming by developing policies and regulations that promote sustainable farming practices and provide incentives to farmers who adopt them. Consumers can support sustainable farming by choosing to purchase products from sustainable farms and by advocating for sustainable farming practices in their communities.

Farmers can also play a key role in educating consumers and policymakers about the benefits of sustainable farming and the challenges they face in implementing sustainable practices. By sharing their experiences and knowledge, they can help build support for sustainable farming and encourage others to adopt these practices.

Policymakers can help support sustainable farming by investing in research and development of sustainable farming technologies, providing funding for sustainable farming programs, and creating policies that promote sustainable farming practices. For example, policies that provide tax incentives or subsidies for sustainable farming practices can help encourage farmers to adopt these practices.

Consumers can also play a key role in promoting sustainable farming by choosing to purchase products from sustainable farms and by advocating for sustainable farming practices in their communities. By supporting sustainable farming practices, consumers can help create a market for sustainably produced products, which can help drive demand for sustainable farming practices and encourage more farmers to adopt them.

VIII. Conclusion

Recap Of Sustainable Farming Principles And Techniques

Sustainable farming involves agricultural practices that prioritize the long-term health and productivity of ecosystems while minimizing negative impacts on the environment. Here is a recap of some of the sustainable farming principles and techniques:

- Minimizing negative impacts on ecosystems
- Biodiversity and crop rotation
- Local adaptation
- Integrated pest management
- Organic farming methods
- Agroforestry

- Conservation tillage
- Drip irrigation
- Grazing techniques that promote biodiversity
- Animal welfare considerations
- Alternative protein sources

These practices vary by region and must be adapted to local circumstances to be effective. They also require collaboration among farmers, policymakers, and consumers to promote sustainable farming practices, address economic, policy, social, and technological challenges, and support a healthy planet for future generations.

Call To Action For Sustainable Farming Practices

As individuals, policymakers, and members of the farming community, we have a responsibility to promote and support sustainable farming practices. This means prioritizing practices that minimize negative impacts on ecosystems, promote biodiversity, and prioritize animal welfare. It also means working to address the economic, social, and policy challenges that can impede the widespread adoption of sustainable farming practices.

As consumers, we can support sustainable farming practices by seeking out sustainably produced food and supporting local farmers who prioritize sustainable practices. As policymakers, we can promote sustainable farming through the development of policies that support sustainable practices and provide economic incentives for farmers who adopt these practices.

As farmers, we can prioritize sustainable farming practices by adopting practices that minimize negative impacts on the environment, promote biodiversity, and prioritize animal welfare. We can also work to educate others about the benefits of sustainable farming and advocate for policies that support sustainable farming practices.

By working together to promote and support sustainable farming practices, we can cultivate a more sustainable future for ourselves, our communities, and our planet.

Final Thoughts On The Importance Of Sustainable Farming For Our Future

In conclusion, sustainable farming practices are crucial for our future. With increasing concerns about food security, climate change, and environmental degradation, it is becoming more and more important to adopt farming practices that preserve and protect our natural resources while also producing healthy and nutritious food. By implementing sustainable farming practices such as agroforestry, conservation tillage, and integrated pest management, we can minimize negative impacts on ecosystems, promote biodiversity, and reduce greenhouse gas emissions.

However, achieving sustainable farming requires collaboration between farmers, policymakers, and consumers. Policymakers can incentivize sustainable practices and support research and development, while consumers can demand sustainably-produced food and support local farmers. Farmers, in turn, can implement sustainable practices on their farms and be active participants in the movement towards a more sustainable future.

In short, sustainable farming is not just important for the health of our planet and its inhabitants, but it is also critical for the long-term viability of our food systems. By working together, we can create a sustainable future for ourselves and for generations to come.